'When This You See Remember Me'

Exhibition at
Witney Antiques

96 - 100 Corn Street, Witney, Oxon OX28 6BU
Telephone : 01993 703902 Fax : 01993 779852
E-mail : witneyantiques@community.co.uk
Website : www.witneyantiques.com

Member of the British Antique Dealers' Association

Acknowledgements

Katherine Barker
Lara Belshah
WK & EM Sessions. Sessions of York
Stephen Williams, Genealogist
Religious Society of Friends in Britain. Library

Photography

Justin Jarrett

Catalogue

Joy and Stephen Jarrett. Rebecca Scott

© **Witney Antiques, 2001**
Published by Witney Antiques
96-100 Corn Street, Witney, Oxfordshire OX28 6BU
Tel : 01993 703902 Fax : 01993 779852

Produced by
David Hewitt Associates

Due to the printing process colours may vary slightly to those of the original samplers.

All rights reserved. No part of this publication may be reproduced, stored in a retrieval system, or transmitted, in any form or by any means, electronic, mechanical, photocopying, recording or otherwise, without the prior permission of the copyright holder.

ISBN 0 9518186 9 4

Foreword

The title of this years exhibition comes from a sampler worked by Charlotte Malpas in 1834.

'When this you see remember me
And bear me in your mind
Let all the world say what they will
Speak of me as you find'.

This verse with numerous variations occurs over and over again on samplers, and always leaves a feeling of curiosity towards the maker. Many such samplers provide us with a remarkable insight into the lives, aspirations and endeavours of generations of young girls. Sometimes worked to be given as gifts or intended to be of permanent interest recording family events, births, deaths, marriages and friendships.

Some of the samplers in this exhibition include the place where they were worked, and through this we are able to build a historical background comparing the change in life between then and now. Green fields long built up, small villages now sprawling commuter towns, rural communities striving for betterment. Grand houses, charity schools, orphanages and an age that lived without our modern conveniences of electricity, telephones and motor cars. Even the fall of family fortunes are reflected. Louisa Golding Chapmans sampler, possibly worked in a small private school, using expensive silk threads, illustrates this when we discover in the 1881 census that her only son, was eighty years old and is recorded as a widowed pauper living in the Union Workhouse, Edgeware Road, London.

Jane Graham's plain sewing sampler worked on unbleached linen in black thread, provides a lasting testament to the austere life led by young girls in Quaker schools, as does that of Esther Wilson who attended Esther Tuke's School in York.

Betsy Cort from Demerara in the West Indies, Hepzibah Hornblower born in 1816, Sarah Duxbury, Rachel Scotcher and Elizabeth Lindo are just a few of the girls whose lives have touched us and are all part of a wonderful legacy of girlhood embroidery.

Every sampler has a story to tell, and their preservation survives as a wonderful memorial to their makers and their young lives.

Also included in the exhibition are a few samplers for which we have been unable to ascertain where they were worked and thus have been unable to search through the appropriate parish records. However they represent the many young girls whose names live on, recorded on their samplers by their own industry and skill.

1. Judith Pycock. 1717.
2. Ann Bainbridge. 1727.
3. Mary Stone. 1739.
4. Ann Sheppard. 1762.
5. Grizel Henderson. Mid 18th Century.
6. Bell Ker. Circa last quarter 18th Century.
7. Mary Ogden. 1783.
8. Ann Blagdon. 1785.
9. Mary Braine. 1787.
10. EW. 1796.
11. Miniature Sampler. 1797.
12. Watch Holder. Early 19th Century.
13. Silk and Wool Embroidery. Early 19th c.
14. Mary Denham. 1802.
15. Harriot Perrin. Circa 1805.
16. Jane Greenberry. 1807.
17. Kensington School. Early 19th Century.
18. Louisa Chapman Golding. 1812.
19. Jane Graham. 1819.
20. Betsy Cort. 1818.
21. Pair of water-colour & silk embroideries. Early 19th Century.
22. Matilda Checkley. 1819.
23. Susey Woolfenden. 1821.
24. Elizabeth Price. 1821.
25. Sarah Bounds. Early 19th Century.
26. M. Elliott. 1822.
27. Hephzibah Hornblower. 1829.
28. Sarah Duxbury. 1829.
29. Rebecca Bradford. 1833.
30. Charlotte Malpas. 1834.
31. Mary Ann Dickerson. 1835.
32. Memorial Sampler. 1836.
33. Memorial Sampler. 1838.
34. Mary Hibbert. 1836.
35. Elizabeth H Hinton. 1837.
36. Elizabeth Rachel Scotcher. 1838.
37. Charlotte Adams. 1839.
38. Elizabeth Ellen Lindo. 1840.
39. Needlework Specimens. Lady Lortons School. 1840.
40. Esther Walker. 1841.
41. Hellen McCubbin. 1843.
42. Elizabeth Lawrance. 1851.
43. Elizabeth Cooper. 1852.
44. Jane Gardiner. 1871.
45. Annie Parker. 1882.

Reverse Side

1. Judith Pycock
1717

Judith Pycock certainly intended her meticulously worked sampler to be a lasting memorial to herself.

*'This work in hand my friends may have
when I am dead and laid in Grave'.*

Worked in band form in coloured silks on an unbleached linen ground with alphabets, border patterns and moralistic verses.

The sampler is reversible, a hall mark of many 17th century and early 18th century samplers, and shows a high degree of proficiency.

2. Ann Bainbridge. 'HER SAMPLER. 1727'

A band sampler worked in coloured silks on linen with alphabets, numerals and moralistic verses.

A broad floral band with rosebuds and a carnation forms a striking image at the bottom edge of the sampler.

Framed Size. 21½" x 11½". 53cm x 29cm.

3. Mary Stone. 'HER WORK FINISHED 1739'.

During the 18th century the use of the Lord's Prayer on samplers became increasingly popular. This beautifully worked example places the text within a central tablet surrounded by flowers.

Coloured silks on wool.

Framed Size. 14½" x 12½". 37cm x 32cm.

4. Ann Sheppard. 1762. Tottenham.

An exceptionally finely embroidered sampler with a large area of carefully worked text, surrounded by a wide floral border which includes freely flowing blossoms of rose, lily, tulip, convolvulus and carnation.

This sampler makes an interesting comparison with a sampler by Mary Nickolls (1755) in the Fitzwilliam Museum, Cambridge.★

In the 18th century Tottenham was almost a separate village from the City of London. As businessmen prospered many families moved out of the teeming streets of London to more pleasant country surroundings.

Ann was the daughter of Joseph Sheppard and Sarah Bruster who were married on July 2nd 1738 at St Mary Magdalene's Church in Old Fish Street. Six children from the marriage are recorded, including Ann who was christened on April 6th 1749 at St Botolph's Without, Aldersgate.

By the age of thirteen her embroidery was already of a very high standard. Eleven years later at the age of twenty four she married William Turvey at the same church in which she was christened. The church registers record the christenings of their children, Rebecca 1773, Elizabeth 1777 and Thomas 1780.

★ No 26. Page 62. Samplers. Carol Humphries.

Framed Size. 21" x 16". 53cm x 41cm.

5. Grizel Henderson. Aged 11. Mid 18th century.

Although this sampler is undated it is almost identical to one by Jean Mvrry which bears the date 1740. Collection of the Royal Scottish Museum, Edinburgh. Ref. 1976.588. Illustration No 12 'Samplers' Naomi Tarrant. Pub. 1978.

Clearly both samplers have been worked under the same instruction and from the same pattern source, although many of the images are familiar on other Scottish samplers.

Worked in coloured silks on wool in cross, double running, stem, back and satin stitch, with the Ten Commandments in two octagonal tablets either side of a baronial building, with a guard in the doorway. Bands of undulating flowers, open-tailed peacocks and birds occupy the top half of the sampler. Small coronets each with a letter denoting a rank, i.e. King, Lord, Viscount, Earl, Duke and Marquis.

In common with many Scottish samplers Grizel has included the names of her parents, James Henderson and Christen Inglees (maiden name). The pairs of initials represent family members, probably siblings.

Framed Size. 16" x 18" 41cm x 46cm.

6. BELL KER
Circa last quarter 18th century.

A fine sampler with typical Scottish elements, worked in silk. Perhaps the most striking feature of this highly accomplished work is the ornamented upper-case alphabet, a hall-mark of many Scottish samplers and probably derived from late Renaissance penmanship. The absence of the letters J and U should also be noted.

The fountain with birds surrounded by a wreath of leaves is another Scottish feature, along with the open-tailed peacock and band of undulating flowers.

Framed Size. 16" x 13½". 41cm x 35cm.

Below :

7. Mary Ogden. 1783. 11 years & 4 months.

Worked on unbleached gauze in coloured silks. Eyelet, cross and satin stitch.

With evident pride Mary Ogden has precisely embroidered her age on completing her sampler. Worked in spot motif form with the Pascal Lamb as the main figurative subject.

Mary was born at Ashton under Lyne (Lancs.) and baptised at St. Michael's Church on August 23rd 1772, daughter of James and Susannah Ogden. James and his wife had seven children. Margaret baptised 1758, John 1760, William 1762, Susannah 1766, Ralph 1767, Ann 1769, Betty (Beth) 1770 and Mary 1772, all are recorded at Ashton.

On the sampler Mary records the names of her parents and five brothers and sisters. Presumably her other siblings died in infancy.

Mary Ogden married James Grimshaw when she was aged twentythree at the church where she was christened. The same register names three children born to union. Sally 1796, Betty 1798 and Mary 1803. The surname Ogden is frequently found in Lancashire.

Framed Size. 24½" x 18½". 62cm x 47cm.

8. Ann Blagdon. 1785. Aged 10 years. South Shields. Co. Durham.

The port of Southshields on the Tyne estuary was one of contrasts, with quays, warehouses and factories along with attractive gardens and large houses. It was here that the Romans built a fort as a supply base for the garrison of Hadrian's Wall and for troops operating north of it.

There was a long tradition of the Blagdon family at South Shields dating at least to Ralph Blagdon (Ann's grandfather) marrying Elizabeth Young at St Hilda's Church on May 18th 1730.

One of their children named after his father married Elizabeth Gibson on the 28th May 1762. Their first child, Mary, is named on the sampler and was born in 1763 as are William and Robert two of Ann's brothers. Other children in the family were Margaret, Elizabeth, Eleanor and a second Margaret.

The sampler worked on an unevenly spun and loosely woven ground in shades of fine red and green wool has a charming naive appeal.

Framed Size. 29" x 17".
74cm x 43cm.

9. Mary Braine. Warkton. 1787.
Taught by Mary Blackburn. Kettering. Northamptonshire.

'SOLOMON'S JUDGEMENT BETWEEN TWO HARLOTS'.

A rare and unusual sampler worked on a silk ground, embroidered with coloured silks, metallic thread, plaited ribbon and applique fabric, with a long biblical text from the Book of Solomon.

Mary Braine came from Warkton, a small village just outside the town of Kettering, which in 1801 had a population of 3011. In a directory for 1791 it is stated '*Here is a free school for all boys belonging to the Parish and a small charity school for girls to read, spin and knit*'. As well as these schools there would also have been a number of small private schools.

We can find no record of Mary Blackburn, school mistress, whose name is recorded for posterity on this interesting sampler.

Framed Size. 30½" x 26". 78cm x 66cm.

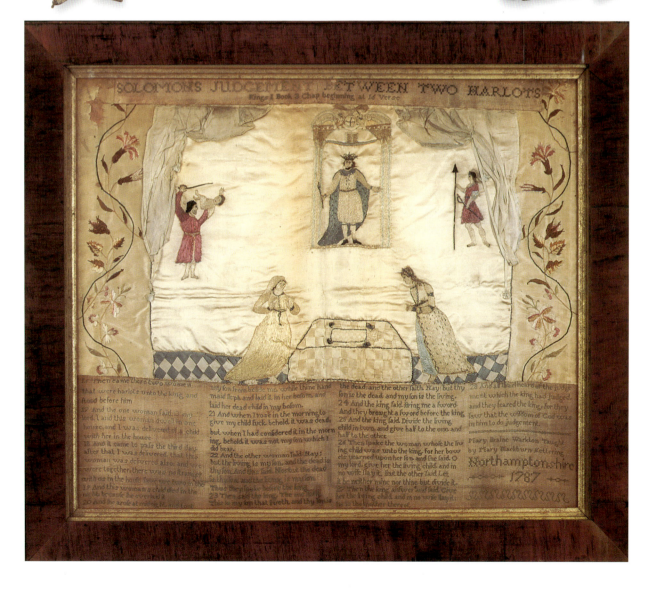

10. EW 1796

This typical Quaker medallion sampler embroidered in blue, green and brown silks on unbleached linen serves as a permanent early record of a school established by the Quaker visionary Esther Tuke.

Coming from a prominent York Quaker family Esther and her husband William Tuke III had been instrumental in raising money and enthusiasm amongst the York Meeting of the Society of Friends for the founding of a Quaker boarding school at Ackworth in 1779. Indeed two of their children Ann (1767- 1849) and Mabel (1770-1864) attended the school from 1780, (Ann for one year and Mabel for four years). Constantly travelling around

1784
PROPOSED
BOARDING - SCHOOL FOR GIRLS
At YORK.

THE Education of Friends Children in general, especially Girls, confistent with the Principles we profefs, having been the fubject of folid confideration with divers Friends, who have beheld with fatisfaction the advantages derived from ACKWORTH SCHOOL, and are defirous that a fimilar opportunity of a guarded Education may be extended to fuch Girls, who, by reafon of their Age, or on account of the circumftances of their Parents or Friends, are not fent thither.

In order to promote an eftablifhment fo beneficial to the Society, the following Friends propose to open a SCHOOL at YORK, viz.

ESTHER TUKE	§	TABITHA MIDDLETON
MARTHA ROUTH	§	SARAH GRUBB
MARY PROUD	§	SARAH SWANWICK
ANN NORTH	§	ELIZABETH HOYLAND
SARAH PRIESTMAN	§	

with a hope that, if the Inftitution is found to anfwer the defired end, other Friends will, after the deceafe of any of them, unite with the Survivors for its continuance and fupport.

The School is intended to be opened the 1ft of 1ft month., 1785, under the immediate infpection of Efther Tuke, and occafionally of others of the aforefaid Friends. Suitable Teachers to be provided for inftructing the Children in ufeful Needlework, Knitting, the Englifh Language, Writing, and Arithmetic.

The terms for Board, Wafhing, and Education, will be 14 Guineas a year, to be paid at Entrance; Wafhing of Gowns and Frocks not included.

None to be taken for lefs than one year; but if any thing extraordinary fhould render their removal neceffary before the expiration of that time, money to be returned for the remaining full quarters.

In order that plainnefs and moderation, confiftent with our religious Principles, may be attended to in the Education of thefe Children, it is requefted that fuch apparel as is coftly, or fuperfluous, may be avoided: alfo fuch kinds as caufe extraordinary trouble in wafhing.

*

the country in order to minister to the Friends, Esther became increasingly driven by the concept of female equality within the society, and, in 1784 Esther helped to establish the first official Womens Yearly Meeting. In the same year Esther together with a group of like minded women proposed that a boarding school for girls be founded at York.

On New Years Day 1785 the school was duly founded at a house in Trinity Lane, off Micklegate, in York. In 1794 Esther Tuke died, but the school continued under the direction of other participating teachers including Esthers daughter Ann, who continued at the school until her marriage in 1796, the year this sampler was worked.

From school enrollment records we can surmise that the initials E W are those of Esther Wilson from Kendal, who was enrolled in the school at number 178 in 1794. From the pairs of initials appearing on the sampler it would seem probable that this sampler was either worked in dedication to her teacher Ann Tuke or as a gift, perhaps as a leaving gift. But for whatever purpose the sampler was worked, in so doing Esther has left behind a permanent record of both pupil and teacher.

This sampler makes an interesting comparison with catalogue nos 16 and 17 from the 1997 exhibition 'Samplers Town and Country', (Witney Antiques) showing two medallion samplers worked at Ackworth school in 1807 and 1811.

Framed Size. 26" x 20". 66cm x 51cm.

★ As printed in 'The Tuke's Of York' by WK & EM Sessions.

Available from Sessions of York. YO31 9HS

Esther (Maud) Tuke

11. Miniature Sampler. 1797.

A charming miniature sampler worked in brightly coloured silks on gauze and bound in green silk ribbon.

Clearly intended as a gift, perhaps to celebrate a marriage, the sampler bears the inscription:

'When you see this rem ember me. The gift is small but love is all'.

Below a pair of co-joined hearts the names *'Mr and Mrs Bur'* are embroidered, clearly the beneficiaries of this delightful memento. Four pairs of initials MD. SP. IH. and AF are placed on alternate sides of a basket of fruit.

Framed Size. 6½" x 8". 16cm x 20cm.

12. Watch Holder. Early 19th Century.

'From the hand of affection'.

The recipient of this charming watch-holder, inscribed *'From the hand of affection'* was possibly unaware that the giver may not have laboured over the gift herself, but instead purchased it from a local charitable institution.

It was not uncommon for the inmates of a work-house or orphanage to put their needle-skills to use by making and embroidering small gifts. Such items were used to raise funds and this charming watch-holder may have been such an example.

Worked in coloured silks on fine gauze, edged and trimmed with silk ribbon.

Framed Size. 10" x 8½". 26cm x 22cm.

13. Silk and Wool Embroidery with Water Colour Detail. Early 19th Century.

'Miss Lightfoot. Princess Risborough'.

The natural progression from sampler making for a well bred young girl was to embroider a silk picture, often worked from a prepared kit, complete with silks and a frame. In contrast, this highly personal embroidery probably depicts the embroideress herself, attired in the height of fashion, in a drawing room elegantly draped with scarlet curtains, and a garden view extending into the distance.

Worked on a linen backed silk mainly in wool with some silk in long and short stitch.

Framed Size. 19" x 22". 48cm x 56cm.

14. Mary Denham. Aged 10 Years
Done at Mrs Shaw's School. St Aubyn Street. (Devon). 1802.

A unique family sampler worked on linen with coloured silks and water colour and silk medallion portraits. The sampler names the children of Henry and Elizabeth Denham, giving details of births, baptisms and burials of family members.

Mary was born at Stoke Damerel, Devon in 1792, the second child of Henry and Elizabeth (Blake), Denham, who had been married at Stoke Damerel Parish Church on August 20th 1789, and was only ten years old when she undertook this ambitious work. Her eight siblings are recorded in the baptismal records of the Parish church and include, Henry (1790), Philip (1793), Catherine (1794), John Blake (1795), Thomas (1796), Richard (1797), James Henry (1798) and George (1800).

According to the 1801 census Stoke Damerel was part of the township of Devonport, whose population at that time was 23,787. No mention is made of Mrs Shaw's School which was probably a private educational establishment catering for a small number of girls and amongst other subjects clearly taught embroidery to a very high standard.

Framed Size. 24" x 23". 61cm x 59cm.

15. Harriot Perrin. Early 19th Century. Circa 1805.

After the Battle of Trafalgar and the death of Admiral Lord Nelson in 1805, the Country was plunged into a period of mourning for her hero who had secured Britain from the threat of invasion by destroying the combined fleets of France and Spain and establishing her command of the seas.

Mourning pictures abounded, poetry was written and samplers worked in schools extolling Nelson's victories. This sampler was probably worked shortly after his death and bears verses *'Suggested by the motto on Lord Nelson's Funeral Car'*, which are placed above a tomb and urn, over which hangs a stylized weeping willow tree which is flanked by two large potted flowering plants.

'The foe destroyed with triumph blest
Victorious Nelson sunk to rest
Amid the battle's roar
And Fame to distant times shall tell
How gallant Nelson conqu'ring fell
To save his native shores ....'

Worked in coloured silks in cross and satin stitch onto a cream wool ground.

Framed Size. 20" x 17½". 51cm x 45cm.

16. Jane Greenberry (Sic)
Croxton Kerrial. May 20th, 1807.

According to parish records Jane was christened at Croxton Kerrial on July 26th 1807, the daughter of William Greenbury and Sarah Brutnell who had been married in 1802 at Waltham on the Wold, Leicester.

The date recorded on the sampler is Jane's birthdate.

Less than ten years before she was born, Croxton Kerrial was described in the 1799 census as consisting of fifty-nine habitable houses and a hovel. There was also a building which had been converted for use as a school in Middle Street where *'only about a dozen poor children were taught'*. This was funded entirely by charities as was the small free school for boys in School Lane. It is possible that Jane was a pupil at the Middle Street Charity School which would certainly have taught needlework as a principal subject.

English villages at this time were very close communities and two other families named Greenbury also lived in the village, providing several cousins, aunts and uncles.

When Jane was twenty she married John Brotherway on the 13th October 1827 at Croxton.

The sampler is meticulously executed in coloured silks on fine wool.

Framed Size. 11½" x 9½". 29cm x 24cm.

17. Kensington School.
Early 19th Century.

A fine miniature sampler worked in red silk on gauze with alphabets, numerals and 'King' 'England' and 'Queen' beneath crowns and Kensington II School.

The school in Kensington High Street was a charity school and was also known as the National School. Designed by Nicholas Hawksmoor and built in 1711-1712 it was demolished in 1878. In 1804 a new girls school was established. Two stone statues of a boy and a girl carved by the mason Thomas Eustace were preserved on the North elevation of the school, now known as St Mary Abbotts School.

Framed Size. 7½" x 8". 19cm x 20cm.

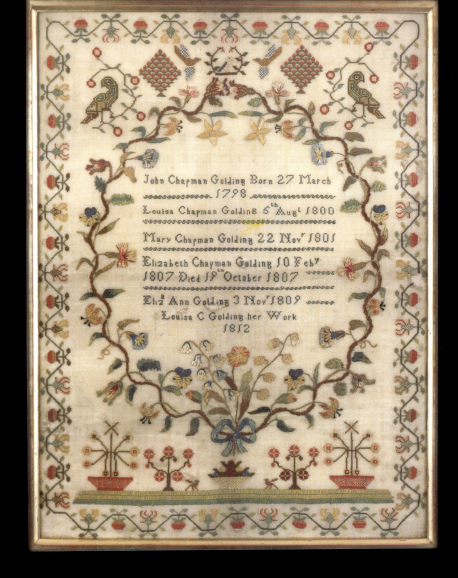

18. Louisa Chapman Golding. Aged 12. 1812.

Geneological samplers can often provide us with a lot of family history and this beautifully worked sampler by twelve year old Louisa Chapman Golding is no exception. According to the sampler Louisa was born on August 5th 1800 but no location is given.

The only name recorded on the sampler, found in parish records is that of her sister Elizabeth Chapman Golding who was baptised in 1807 at St James's Church, Westminster, and who died eight months later. All the children named on the sampler with the exception of Elizabeth Ann (Born 1809) have been given the middle name of Chapman which may have been an earlier family name. Their parents marriage took place at St Dunstan in the East, London, when Robert Golding married Maria Glasscock on July 4th 1795.

In 1821, when Louisa was 21 years old she married John Dely Barnes, on September 16th at Christ Church, Grey Friars, Newgate. One child to this union was born. John Golding Barnes, baptised 13th September 1822 at St Leonard's Eastcheap.

In contrast to the rich and expensive silks with which Louisa worked her sampler we find that her son some sixty-nine years later according to the 1881 census was living at the Union Workhouse, Edgeware Road, London, listed as an 82 year old widower and pauper.

Provenance. Miss Carrie Neely. Chicago

Collection Museum of Science and Industry, Chicago. 1939-1998.

Exhibited. Millenium Exhibition. National Maritime Museum, Greenwich, London.

'The Story of Time'. Exhibit 268.

Framed Size. 21½" x 17". 55cm x 43cm.

19. Jane Graham. Wigton School (Cumberland) 1819.

A simple Quaker school sampler, by Jane Graham, Wigton School, worked in black thread on coarse linen ground, in cross stitch.

Wigton School was opened at Highmoor, Wigton, Cumberland on 4th September 1815 with 9 boys and 8 girls. Although by 1819, the date of Jane's sampler, the numbers had increased to 15 boys and 15 girls. The school founded by the Cumberland Friends did however take the children of non Quakers, so long as the child was *'brought up in an orderly manner and was in frequent attendance of their own religious meetings'*.★

Jane Graham, born in Wigton in 1809, was one such pupil, being baptised at the local church on the 23rd July 1809. It seems probable that Jane's parents John Graham and Mary Scot originated from north of the border, and from local records we know that the family moved from Wigton to Maryport (on the Solway Firth) for some years between 1809 and 1819. On the 18th October 1813 Jane was re-baptised at the Scottish Presbyterian Church, as were her two siblings Thomas

Wigton School

and Elizabeth. However within a few years the family had returned to Wigton where Jane attended school.

Jane's sampler was worked under the instruction of Elizabeth Mason from York who was employed at Wigton to teach girls *'reading, writing, English grammar, arithmetic, geography, sewing and knitting'*. School life was hard, the girls rose at 6 o'clock each morning and as well as completing their school work they were expected to *'sweep and dust the school and lodging rooms, to make up and repair their own and the boys linen, clean their shoes, make all beds, wait at table, assist in the kitchen and on all other domestic duties decided upon by the committee'*.★

Jane's simple school sampler serves as a lasting testament to Quaker school girl education, and makes an interesting comparison with that produced at Esther Tuke's school in York some 22 years earlier. (See Cat. No.10).

★ 1815-1953. Friends School. Wigton. Cumberland.

Ed. D.W. Reed. Pub. Wigton Old Schools Ass. 1954.

Framed Size. 12" x 13".
30cm x 33cm.

20. Betsy Cort. 16 May 1818.
Demerary. (Guiana, West Indies).

A very rare embroidered letter by Betsy Cort of Demerary, to Mrs Wilson, worked in minute cross stitch in scarlet thread on a linen ground.

'DEAR MRS WILSON
                    AS I CANNOT WRITE TO YOU I HOPE YOU WILL
NOT THINK I FORGET ALL YOUR KINDNESS TO ME. I NEVER CAN BE SO
UNGRATEFUL. MANY THANKS FOR THE GOWN BY DAVID BETHUNE AND
PRAY THANK MRS POWELL FOR THE RING. I HOPE YOUR HEALTH IS NOW
MENDING FAST AND MR WILSON'S. YOU HAVE MADE US ALL SORRY TO HEAR
WE SHALL NOT SEE YOU AGAIN. EVERY BODY HERE WISHES YOU WELL AND DID
NOT THINK YOU AND MR WILSON WOULD HAVE LEFT US TO REMAIN IN ENGLAND.
BUT I HOPE THAT IT IS ALL FOR YOUR GOOD. GOD BLESS YOU. PRAY REMEMBER ME MOST
KINDLY TO MISS ELIZA AND HER BROTHER, MRS CORT'S FAMILY AND PATIENCE
AND YOUR SISTERS.   I AM
                          DEAR MRS WILSON
                          YOUR OBLIGED
DEMERARY   BETSY CORT.'
16 MAY 1818.

By word of mouth Mrs Wilson is believed to have been a missionary during the early 19th century in Demerara, however searches so far have failed to establish this. This intriguing letter does serve to remind us of life in this West Indian colony and the many missionaries who went out to 'bring consolation of religion' to the slaves.

Slaves in Demerara were amongst the most exploited in the region and the establishment of black churches provided a meeting place where slaves from different plantations could get together for gossip and friendship, eventually leading to the slave revolt in 1823. The Rev John Smith from the London Missionary Society was held responsible for the outbreak and sentenced to hang, whilst two hundred and fifty slaves were brutally slain and their dismembered bodies put on public display.★

★ 'Black Ivory, A History of British Slavery' James Walvin.   Framed Size. 11½" x 8". 29cm x 20cm.

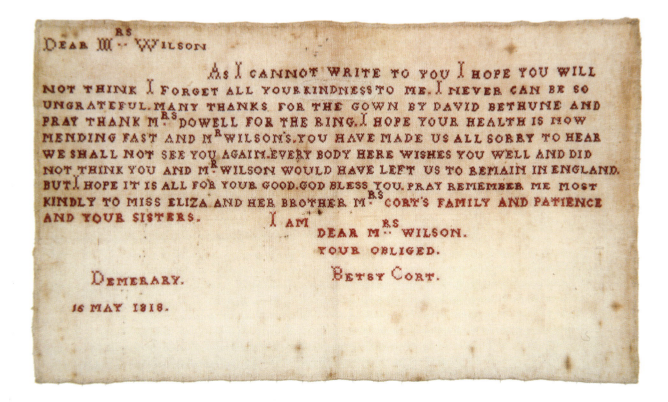

21. Pair of water-colour and silk embroideries. Artist unknown. Early 19th Century.

This pair of rare and striking 'missionary' images worked by an unknown hand, are like Betsy Cort's letter to Mrs Wilson, wonderfully evocative.

Missionaries travelled throughout the world including the Pacific Islands and the slave colonies of North America and the West Indies to preach their dream of 'the salvation to come'. Here the two missionaries are poertrayed wearing tight fitting trousers and jackets, both ill suited to hot foreign climes.

Framed Size. 19½" x 17". 49cm x 43cm.

22. Matilda Checkley. Daventry (Northamptonshire). 1819.

An attractive small sampler worked in coloured silks by ten year old Matilda Checkley probably whilst at school in Daventry.

Records show that Matilda was born and baptised in 1809 at Sheaf Street Independent Chapel, Daventry, the daughter of William and Rebecca (Cook) Checkley, who were married at All Saints Church, Northampton on October 30 1798.

According to Piggots 1824 Directory of Northampton, her father William is listed as one of nineteen butchers in the town with premises at St Sepulchre's, Church Lane.

Framed Size. 17½" x 16".
45cm x 41cm.

23. Susey Woolfenden. 1821.

A rare sampler probably worked as a school-room exercise recording the life of Margaret Scot, who reputedly lived for one hundred and twenty-five years!

Worked in coloured silks on linen.

Framed Size. 20" x 20".
51cm x 51cm.

Private Collection.

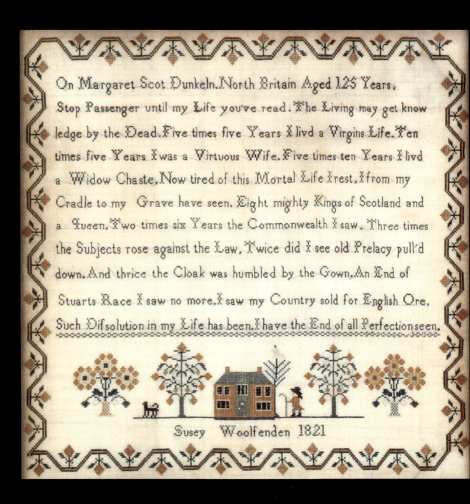

24. Elizabeth Price. 1821.

The year in which this sampler was worked saw the death of Queen Caroline and the coronation of King William IV.

This delightful and unusual sampler is worked in coloured silks on cream wool. The central composition of a house with weeping willow trees is encircled by an oval meandering border of flowers which springs to life from a sheaf of corn embroidered on the bottom edge.

Framed Size. 27" x 25½". 69cm x 65cm.

25. Sarah Bounds. Early 19th Century.

By contrast to the freely worked sampler by Elizabeth Price, Sarah's sampler is faultlessly embroidered with symetrical mirror images. It's stylistic format is representative of numbers of samplers worked during the 19th century, involving the painstaking counting of threads (in itself a mathematical exercise) to achieve the exacting composition.

Silk on cream wool.

Framed Size. 21" x 16". 54cm x 41cm.

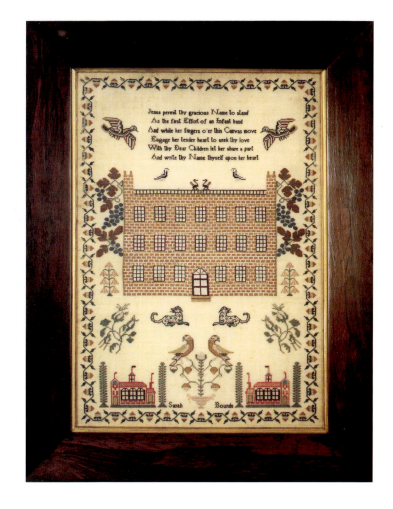

26. M. Elliott.
June 30th 1822.

A remarkable collection of needlework by the same hand, comprising a watch holder, watch glass cover and three samplers.

Whilst needlework was the foundation stone of female education and an important leisure activity for daughters of the middle classes, samplers were worked by all strata of society. Some of the finest work to survive is that produced by the poorest girls in the most adverse conditions. For the daughters of the poor and orphans in particular, being skilled with a needle was a passport to a better life.

The back of one of the pieces bears the poignant inscription

'Ever generous kind and true
To all who need his care
But still to none so kind and true
As to the orphan child'.

That these unique pieces should have remained together for almost two hundred years in such fine condition is indeed remarkable and is a tribute not only to the young embroideress but also to the many thousands of anonymous disadvantaged children of 19th century Britain.

Framed Size. 22" x 23". 56cm x 58cm.

27. Hephzibah Hornblower. 1829.

Hephzibah's unusual name has enabled us to find her birth records without the help of a known location. Her parents were Benjamin and Sarah Hornblower of Catshill, Bromsgrove, Worcestershire, who had their daughter christened on 31st March 1816. Their other living children were William (1805) Jeremiah (1806) Issac (1807) Mary Ann (1809) Eliza (1811) and Joshua (1818). In the census of 1821 their father is listed as a labourer but, by the 1851 census, her brother Joshua, now 32 years old, is a farmer with ten acres.

As was quite common during the 19th century many fore-names were taken from the Old Testament. Hephzibah being Hebrew in origin, means charmingly 'in her is my delight' alluding to a new born daughter.

The sampler worked in coloured silks has as its centre piece a large church with pointed steeple and circular turret clock divided into quarters and a two line text:

'If all mankind would dwell in mutual love
This world would much resemble that above'.

Where Hephzibah received her education is uncertain but Bromsgrove boasted several girls schools. Listed in the 1820 Lewis's Worcestershire General and Commercial Directory are Mrs Hall's School and Mrs Heywood's, both in the High Street and Mrs Pinches in St John's Street.

Framed Size. 21½" x 19". 55cm x 48cm.

28. Sarah Duxbury. 1829.

'Sarah Duxbury to the memory of her Dear Brother who died Aug 8. 1823'.

A brightly coloured sampler worked in fine wools by Sarah Duxbury in memory of her brother whose initials J.D mark a flower-adorned tomb, and who died six years earlier.

This sampler is in direct contrast to the sombre and anonymous memorial piece to William Cunliffe (1836) worked entirely in black thread. Cat. No.32.

When blooming youth is snatch'd away
By death resistless hand
Our hearts the mournful tribute pay
Which pity must demand

Let this vain world engage no more
Behold the gaping tomb
It bids us seize the present hour
To morrow death may come'.

Framed Size. 15½" x 13". 39cm x 33cm.

29. Rebecca Bradford. 1833.

Clearly a school-room lesson combining practice in plain sewing, with rows of alphabets and numerals, moralistic maxims and a short history lesson.

Through this sampler the young King Edward VI, who lived for only 16 years (1537-53) and an anonymous, poor woman are remembered. Edward, the son of Henry VIII and Jane Seymour, developed into a studious but sickly youth, whose education from the age of six years was entrusted to Richard Cox. At his succession to the throne at the age of ten his uncle Edward Seymour was chosen as Lord Protector and it was he who caused the King to sign a death warrant for the execution of a poor woman on account of her religious principles, and to make the tearful and poignant remark, 'I almost wish I had never learned to write'.

'Edward the sixth, king of England, being
when very young, required by his uncle
to sign a warrant for the execution of
a poor woman, on account of her religi-
ous principles, said, with tears in his eyes:
I almost wish I had never learned to
                write'.

Silk on cream wool.

Framed Size. 15" x 19". 38cm x 49cm.

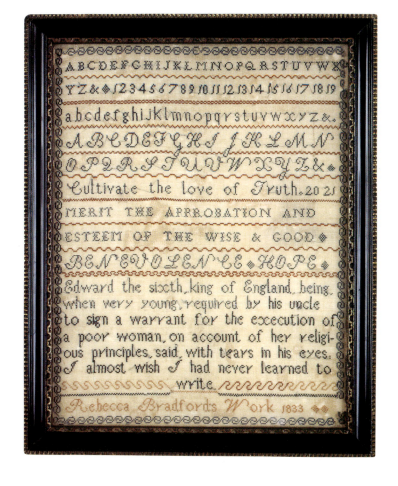

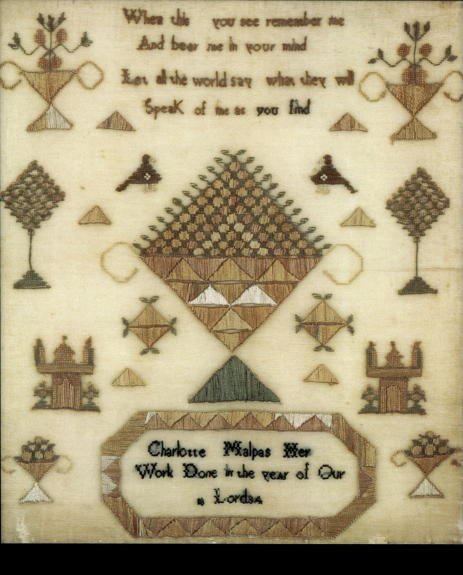

30. Charlotte Malpas
1834.

'When this you see remember me
And bear me in your mind
Let all the world say what they will
Speak of me as you find'.

Charlotte Malpas has left an endearing message to posterity that she should be remembered through her sampler. Carefully worked in coloured silks on fine gauze in cross and satin stitch, it stands as a tribute to her embroidery skills.

This sampler should be compared with a sampler by Emma Ware in the collection of Bristol City Museum and Art Gallery. Illustrated. 'Samplers' Karin Walton, Page 47. Fig.61.

Framed Size. 13½" x 14½". 34cm x 37cm.

31. Mary Ann Dickerson. March 8th 1835. Glenarm. Scotland.

This sampler is representative of many samplers worked between 1830 and 1845, in both the selected colour palette, a profusion of many small motifs and the ubiquitous figures of Adam and Eve. Along with the usual moralistic text, Mary has selected a short poem entitled 'Forget me not'. This poem is reminiscent in it's sentimentality to the thoughts frequently expressed in Victorian novelettes. The romantic notion of parted lovers and a plea to *'Forget me not'*.

*'To flourish round my native bower and
Blossom near my cot I cultivate a little
Flower they call Forget me not.*

*Though oceans may betwixt us roar
And distant be our lot. Ah though we
Part to meet no more dear youth
Forget me not'.*

Glenarm Farmhouse Scotland 2001.

Glenarm is situated at the foot of Glen Cova (Angus, Scotland) and is a long established farm-house, which is still inhabited today. According to the earliest census of 1841, the farm Glenarm was owned by Alexander Ogilvy and his son David, who most likely would have been cattle farmers breeding Aberdeen Angus. They had six servants and labourers including a Betty Dickson (Dickerson probably being a variant spelling) aged 60, whose trade is given as a stocking weaver. It would seem likely that she was a relative of Mary Ann, possibly grandmother or aunt and that Mary Ann was living with her at Glenarm in 1835.

The local parish school was at Cortachy and it may have been here that Mary Ann received an elementary education which would have included sewing and the making of this sampler.

Framed Size. 22" x 17".
56cm x 43cm.

32. Memorial Sampler. 1836.

A simple memorial sampler worked in cross stitch with black thread on unbleached linen.

'In Memory
of William Cunliffe
the son of John and Mary Cunliffe
Who died on 23 of June
1836'.

Many samplers worked by a family member or friend were intended as a permanent personal memorial to the departed. At times the Victorian attitude to death could be maudlin.

'*A fair and lovely flower
On earth it bloomed to fade
In heaven t'will bloom for ever*'.

Framed Size. 11" x 11". 28cm x 28cm.

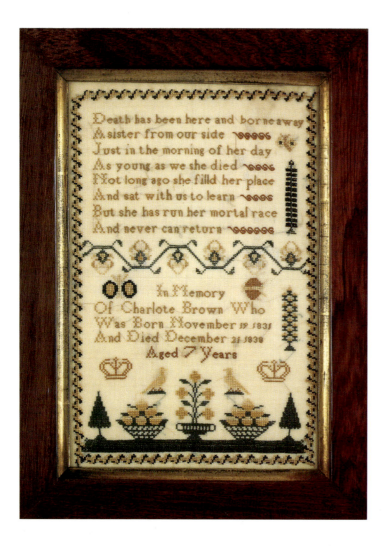

33. Memorial Sampler. 1838.

The memory of seven year old Charlotte Brown has been perpetuated through this charming small sampler worked by one of her sisters.

Death was no stranger to the average family a hundred and fifty years ago, and children were not shielded from the grim realities of life. Diseases such as cholera, typhus, smallpox etc. were never far away and children accepted the fact of early death, shown in such verses as are embroidered on this sampler.

'*Death has been here and bourne away
A sister from our side
Just in the morning of her day
As young as us she died
Not long ago she filld her place
And sat with us to learn
But she has run her mortal race
And never can return*'.

Silk on cream wool.

Framed Size. 10" x 14". 25cm x 36cm.

34. Mary Hibbert.
'finished this work December 21st 1836'.

An appealing sampler worked in fine wools on linen, devoted to one generation of the Hibbert family, recording the names of the children of

'John Hibbert. Born March 7. 1795.
Mary Hibbert. Born April 28. 1795'.

Research has shown that the Hibbert family came from the Manchester area. John Hibbert from Crowthorn near Dukinfield and his eventual wife, Mary Crooks from Walmsley, both families were Presbyterians. However on April 18th 1813 the couple were married at Manchester Cathedral, a popular place for marriages with large numbers taking place on the same day.

Recorded on the sampler are the names of their children with their dates of birth and, according to this register, Mary had her first child at the age of twenty two and continued bearing children until she reached the age of forty two.

All their children were christened at St Michael's, Ashton-under-Lyne with the exception of their eldest child, Mary, who was baptised at Droylesden.

It will be noticed on the sampler three little girls named Elizabeth are recorded.

'Elizabeth Hibbert Born Aug 27. 1825
Died January 22 1827.
Elizabeth Hibbert Born February 3 1829
Died October 10 1831
Elizabeth Hibbert Born April 30 1833.

In many large families the death of an infant born during the early years of a marriage is followed by the birth of another given the same name.

It was Mary and John's eldest daughter who worked this sampler at the comparatively late age of 21. It was completed four months after her own marriage to Samuel Stockport on 29th August 1836 at her home Parish Church of St Michael's. Ashton-under-Lyne.

Framed Size. 25" x 19". 63cm x 48cm.

35. Elizabeth H Hinton. 1837.
Chapel of Ease to St Mary Magdalene. Islington.

To cater for the huge increase in the population of Islington during the late 18th and early 19th centuries, a Chapel of Ease to the Parish Church of St Mary Magdalene was erected between 1812 and 1814.

Designed by the architect William Wickings the handsome neo-classical building is depicted on Elizabeth's sampler. Erected on the south side of Holloway Road on a spacious plot of land the church incurred enormous expenses, the trustees borrowing a larger amount of money than they were authorised to raise by act of parliment.

Elizabeth was the daughter of George and Mary Hinton of 1 Pleasant Place, Holloway. (Their initials GH and MH appearing in the top left and right hand corners of the sampler). George appears in the 1846 Post Office London Directory at that address as a china and glass dealer, however, in the 1852 Directory it would appear that George may have died as only his wife is listed as carrying on the business. Other Hinton's ran the Highbury Barn Public House.

Academies of all types flourished in this fashionable area for the education of young ladies and gentlemen and it was probably at one of these that Elizabeth worked her fine sampler which also includes the initials of her siblings. C.H., H.H., S.H., J.H.

The format of the sampler itself is extremely sophisticated with architectural detail and perspective, probably taken from a contemporary engraving, showing the burial ground and a row of fashionable terraced houses in the background.

Worked in coloured silks on a wool ground using a variety of stitches including cross, chain, satin and long and short stitch.

Framed in a broad rosewood contemporary frame.

Framed Size. 17" x 16". 43cm x 40cm.

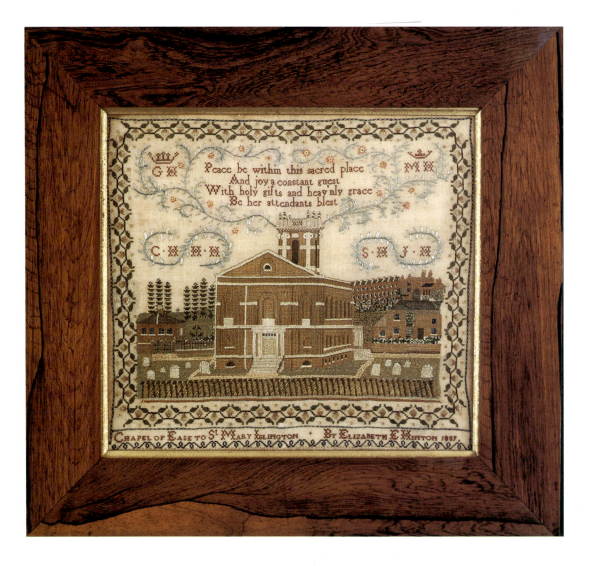

36. Elizabeth Rachel Scotcher. Aged 11. 1838.

This striking and unusual sampler is a poignant reminder to us of the vulnerability of life in the 19th century.

Elizabeth was born and baptised on September 16th 1827 at St Leonard's Church, Shoreditch, London, the only daughter of William and Rachel (Seward) Scotcher. Within a few years of Elizabeth's birth her mother died and William with a young daughter to bring up married again. He and his new wife Elizabeth (Lowe) together produced a further five children.

Sadly only two years after completing her sampler and whilst the family were living in Mile End, London, Elizabeth died aged thirteen. The cause of death, bilious fever.

Worked in brightly coloured silks with the addition of paper details.

Framed Size. 20" x 16". 51cm x 40cm.

Private Collection.

Death Certificate

37. Charlotte Adams. Aged 13 Years 1839.
Donnington Castle.

Charlotte's sampler was worked with the two-fold purpose of combining the learning of embroidery with that of local history in the same way as map samplers combined rudimentary geography and embroidery.

We believe that Charlotte was baptised at West Wycombe Church on July 26th 1826. She was the seventh child of ten surviving children born to William and Ann (Hillsdon) Adams, who were married at the same church on October 12th 1812, when William was only seventeen years old.

It would appear that the family prospered and Charlotte was sent to school in Newbury. At that time Newbury was a flourishing market town with Donnington Castle in it's environs. There were a large number of schools which included 'Ladies boarding and day academies' as well as a Lancastrian National School, Charity and a Bluecoat School. It was probably at one of the small fashionable private schools that Charlotte received her education and worked her sampler.

Silks on a wool ground worked mainly in cross stitch.

Framed Size. 21½" x 17½". 55cm x 45cm.

38. Elizabeth Ellen Lindo.
Aged 11 Years.
1840.

By the time Elizabeth Lindo had reached the age of eleven years her father was dead and she had embroidered this exquisitely stitched and exactingly worked sampler in his memory.

Still retaining the brilliant colouring and worked with a variety of stitches it is a tribute to her unknown teacher and to her own needlework skills.

Framed Size. 16" x 20". 41cm x 51cm.

To the Fatherlefs.
When on the Bed of Death,
My Father laid his head;
To me, with his expiring breath
These words of love he said:
"My dear, my darling girl,
Blessings to thee be given,
Comfort, peace and heavenly joy,
Farewell, we meet in heaven".

59. Specimens of Needlework Executed by the Girls In Lady Lortons School. Boyle. 1840.
Boyle. County Roscommon. Ireland.

This delightful book of needlework specimens includes miniature dresses, kid gloves, stockings and under garments and serves to remind us of life in a typical Irish town during the first half of the 19th century.

Lord and Lady Lorton were wealthy and distinguished landowners in the Boyle area during the 18th and 19th centuries, employing John Nash in 1810 to design their new house in Rockingham demesne.

By contrast to the Lorton's wealth there was much poverty in the area. *'Tenements were to be seen here in the year 1830, of a description so vile, that doubts might well be entertained, if they could be occupied at all by human beings; and certain am I, that in some countries, such places would be considered too wretched for the meanest of domestic animals: bent in roofs, seemingly ready to give way; ragged and leaky thatch; crumbling damp walls over grown with litchens; green without and black within; from the soot deposited by volumnes of turf smoke which before it can find an exit through the door, rolls around the hovel, involving all things in one common obscurity'.* ★

Along with many landowning families the Lorton's were of a charitable disposition, Lady Lorton herself supporting a large girls school in Boyle, where needlework was an important subject on the curriculum. Plain sewing was taught as a possible means of self support and essential to a home maker. As well as many schools in England, Irish schools followed the same system of regulations respecting the teaching of needlework formed on the Madras System, as taught by Dr Bell's Manual of Instruction. (1827) or the British System described in a seventeen page embroidered book worked at Colerain, Ireland.★★

★ Statistical survey of the county of Roscommon. Issac Weld. 1832.

Referring to the quarter of Boyle known as Irish Town.

★★ American Needlework Treasures. Betty Ring. Pages 55-57.

Framed Size. 15" x 12". 38cm x 30cm. (20 pages).

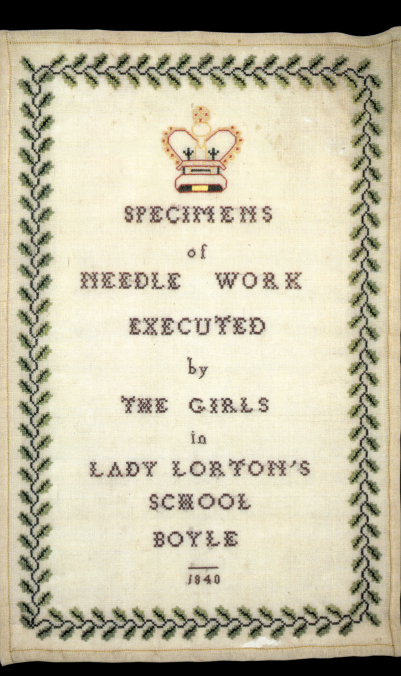

40. Esther Walker. 1841.

'Her work done in Mr Raines Asylum in The Year of Our Lord 1841'.

The term asylum or hospital sometimes found on samplers generally applies to a charity school. Founder of Raines Charity Schools, Henry Raine was a wealthy brewer and pious churchman from Wapping, East London. His first schools were based in the Wapping / Stepney area of London and opened in 1716. They accommodated fifty boys and fifty girls, run by a Master and Mistress, in Charles St. Old Gravel Lane.

In 1736 Raine's Asylum, or Hospital, was established nearby as a boarding school for forty girls, here the girls were trained by a Matron for four years in order to take up domestic service on leaving. The girls were selected after two years elementary education at the charity school founded in 1719. The schools were funded by donations, charity sermons and stock from the South Sea Company and provided board and clothing for the girls as well as £210 anually for two marriage portions and two wedding festivals. The marriage portion was available to past pupils of Raine's Asylum aged 22 years or over, who could produce certificates of good character from former teachers, and whose husbands were suitable members of the Church of England. On May 1 and December 26 each year up to six candidates drew lots from a casket held in the school for marraige portions of £100, hence the nickname the 'Hundred Pound School'.

Other known samplers include one by Mary Kelly of 'Mr Raine's Hospital' 1762. (Sold Christies July 2001).

Esther's unusual sampler demonstrates various darning techniques (an essential skill required for domestic service) using a variety of stitches. Amongst the painstakingly worked verses we read:

'Our term of time is seventy years
An age that few survive
But if with more than common strength
To eighty we arrive'.

Framed Size. 19" x 21". 48cm x 53cm.

Further details of Raine's Charity Schools are held by London Metropolitan Archives, 40 Northampton Road London EC1R 0HB.

41. Hellen McCubbin. 1843.

A sampler by Elizabeth Jenkins, worked at McKenzies School, St Ninians in 1836★ led us to believe that this sampler by Hellen McCubbin, dated 1843 may have been worked at the same school, so strong were the similarities of design.

Although we were unable to locate a birth or baptismal entry, we did find that Helen McCubbin married David Galaghan on 30th July 1848 at St Ninians with further church entries for the baptisms of their children, John and Elizabeth.

The two samplers yet again illustrate that many schools were working identifiable designs which can be linked and attributed to specific schools.

★ Lot 922. Phillips. Scottish Sale. Edinburgh. August 2001.

Framed Size. 29" x 27". 74cm x 68cm.

42. Elizabeth Lawrance. 1851. Adelaide, Australia.

When Elizabeth's grandmother Jane Lawrance received this simple sampler worked as a gift from her grand-daughter, thousands of miles away in Australia, she must have felt many mixed emotions. Joy in the gift and sorrow that she might never see those loved family members again.

Elizabeth's grandfather, Benjamin Lawrance, married Jane Hockin at Falmouth Church on January 28th 1813. Following their marraige they settled in Mylor Churchtown, a small village on a sheltered creek two miles from Falmouth. St Mylor's Church records show the names of their children as they appear on the sampler, plus another daughter Jane who may have died in infancy.

From the 1851 census of Mylor, Benjamin was still living in the village. There is however no mention of brothers John and Joseph who by this time had probably emigrated to Australia.

Further research by the South Australian Genealogy and Heraldry Society Inc. found the marriage of Elizabeth aged twenty, daughter of Joseph Lawrance, to Job Clark aged twenty four at Mount Gambier, South Australia.

A further search in South Australian records children of this couple :-

David born 25.4.1864 at Allendale
Annie born 4.5.1866 at Port McDonnell
Benjamin Joseph born 20.5.1868 at Allendale
Amos born 25.6.1870 at Mount Gambier
Aquala born 21.5.1874 at Mayurra
Job born 20.9.1875 at Hundred of Mt Muirhead
Peter born 16.6.1877 at Hundred of Mt Muirhead
Alfred born 20.5.1879 at Beachport
Elizabeth Wilmott born 13.6.1881 at Beachport
Alice born 10.8.1883 at Beachport

All these places are in the South East of South Australia.

Elizabeth Wilmott CLARK died 26.3.1914 aged 70 years widow of late Job CLARK of Kalangadoo. The certificate states she was born in Paramatta in NSW, that she married aged 20 and then had 6 sons and 2 daughters living and 2 sons and 1 daughter deceased when she died. The cause of death was carcinoma of the colon.

Job CLARK died 24.6.1912 aged 72 years at Kalangadoo. The certificate states he was born in Gloucestershire, town unknown and lived in Australia for 59 years. He was 23 at marraige and the same reference to children was given as that of Elizabeth. Cause of death morbus cordis.

Both Elizabeth and Job are buried in Lake Terrace Cemetery Mount Gambier on 29th March 1914 and 26th June 1912 respectively. There is no headstone.

Although their death certificates state that there were 11 children, we have only been able to find 10 children registered in South Australia. As Mount Gambier is not far from the border with Victoria it is possible that this 11th child was registered there.

Framed Size. 19" x 15".
48cm x 38cm.

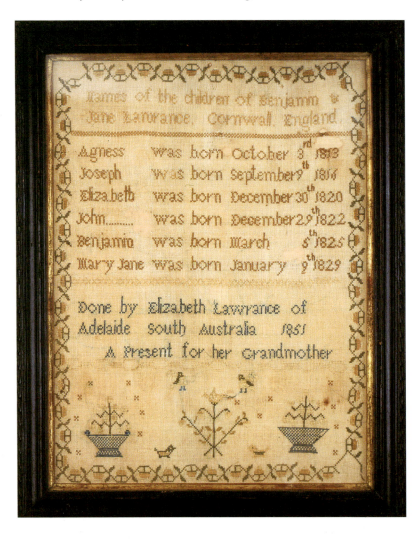

43. Elizabeth Cooper.
Lowestoft Girls School. 1852.

The sampler, although worked in silk shows the influence of the very popular Berlin woolwork patterns. Many of these patterns were given away with such magazines as 'The Young Ladies Journal' and 'The Ladies Treasury'. Through the use of shading, such realistic results could be achieved as seen on the floral border surrounding the sampler, and on the two pairs of mirror images of stags and dogs. It is tempting to imagine Carlo and Juno were indeed family pets.

Lowestoft, in the county of Suffolk, was largely a community where the majority of residents were sailors, fishermen or plied some associated trade. By contrast Elizabeth's father, John Cooper, was listed as a tailor in the 1851 census, although her grandfather who lived with the family at Lighthouse Hill, had nautical connections as a twine spinner.

The school where Elizabeth worked her sampler was probably a free school based on the 'national plan' founded by the Rev Cunningham, who was well known for his philanthropy in nineteenth century Lowestoft. Situated in the High Street it was also known as Cunningham School and later as St Margaret's National Girls' School.

Framed Size. 22" x 17". 56cm x 43cm.

44. Jane Gardiner. 1871.
(Baptised 8th May 1856).

Chewton Mackrell. (Somerset).

By her legacy of girlhood needlework Jane Gardiner left us an interesting glimpse into life in a small Somerset village in the mid 19th century.

Jane's father was a thatcher and as such was a valuable member of the village community. He was presented with awards for the fact that through his hard work he was able to bring up ten children without any help from the parish. Unusual in those times and a fact of which he must have been proud.

Born in Charlton Mackrell in 1816 his first marriage was to Mary Pribeck on January 20th 1839. Three girls were born before Mary died in 1844 and with young children to raise Joseph quickly found another bride and married Caroline Webber on 2nd November 1845. A number of children followed in quick succession, Albert 1846, Francis 1848, John 1849, Ann 1851, Emily 1853, George 1854, Jane 1856, Louise 1858 and Elizabeth 1859. Two other births are recorded giving a total of twelve children, two who did not survive infancy.

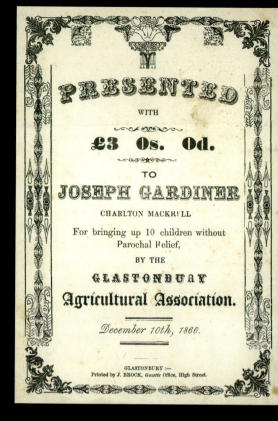

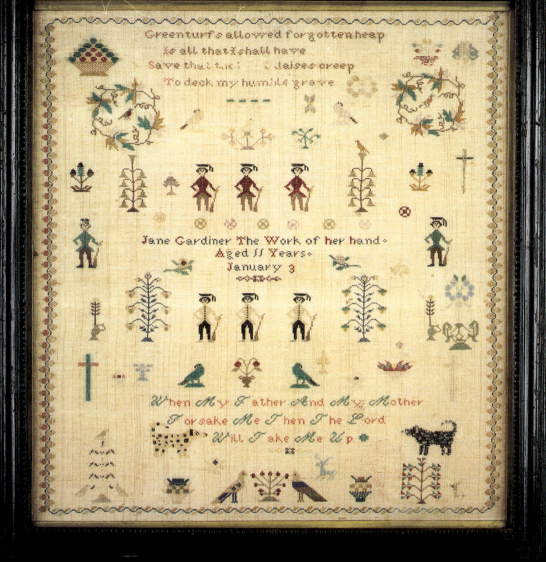

Needlework prizes dated 1869 were won by Elizabeth, Charlotte and Jane who all were attending the local village school. The fact that Jane was still attending school at the age of thirteen bears tribute to Joseph's hard work and obvious belief in the value of education even for the female members of his large family.

45. Annie Parker. 1882.
Hair Sampler 'Presented by her to R.E.Roberts Esquire, Governor'.

A rare hair sampler worked by Annie Parker and presented to R.E. Roberts Esquire, the Governor of Bedford Jail whilst she was a prisoner there. Another sampler was presented the same year by Annie to his daughter Miss D.A.Roberts. Other known examples of her remarkable work include a pin cushion worked in hair, (Black Museum, Scotland Yard) and a sampler in the collection of H.M.Prison Service, (Newbold Revel, near Rugby). A fourth example is illustrated in 'Samplers. Upstairs, Downstairs. Plain and Fancy' published Witney Antiques, Catalogue No.53.

An article from the Daily Chronicle of 22 August 1885 'Death of a Notorious Woman' describes the life of Annie Parker whose death had just taken place at Greenwich Infirmary.

"The death has just taken place in Greenwich Union Infirmary, of Annie Parker, aged 35, who has been over 400 times charged before the magistrates at Greenwich Police Court with drunkeness but never with felony, and has spent the greater part of her life in prison. The cause of her death was consumption. She was always exceedingly well conducted in prison. She has a luxuriant head of hair and whilst in prison worked a number of samplers to give as gifts. These samplers were worked with her own hair, and are unbelievably fine".

"Annie Parker was well educated and a bad word never escaped her. On one occasion a lady took her to Canada, with a view to her reformation, this failed as she could never refuse an intoxicating drink. On the morning of her death, she presented to a Dr Dixon, the assistant medical officer of the Infirmary, a laced edged sampler which was again worked with her own hair".

Framed Size. 17" x 22". 43cm x 56cm.

Witney Antiques Textile Collection.

At our showrooms in Witney we probably hold the largest stock of antique needlework samplers for sale in the country.
With between sixty and one hundred samplers on display a visit is always worthwhile. This stock may be viewed at any time in our specialist department and also during the period of this special exhibition.
We also stock 17th century raised and silk work textiles and 18th century silk pictures.

Since this catalogue went to press we have acquired other samplers which will be included in the exhibition.

Catalogues Available by Post from Witney Antiques.

An 'A - Z of British 18th and 19th Century Samplers'
A general collection of antique needlework samplers.

Samplers. 'A School Room Exercise'
A collection of antique needlework samplers recording the school, institution or teacher under whose instruction the sampler was made.

Samplers. 'House and Garden'
A collection of antique needlework samplers depicting the British house and garden.

Samplers. 'All Creatures Great And Small'
A collection of antique samplers themed around animals, birds and insects.

Samplers. 'Town and Country'
A collection of antique samplers naming the towns and villages in which they were worked.
Including a collection of rare map samplers.

Samplers and Historic Embroideries. 'How Fragrant the Rose'. 1660 - 1860.

British Samplers and Historic Embroideries.
'Upstairs-Downstairs. Plain and Fancy'. 1590 - 1880.

British Samplers and Historic Embroideries.
'Paradise Revisited'. 1590 - 1880.

Samplers and Historic Embroideries.
'When This You See Remember Me'.